Who Was William Shakespeare?

WILLIAM SHAKESPEARE

Who Was William Shakespeare?

By Celeste Davidson Mannis
Illustrated by John O'Brien

Grosset & Dunlap

To Sammie, of course!—C.D.M.
To Tess—J.O.

GROSSET & DUNLAP
Published by the Penguin Group
Penguin Group (USA) Inc., 375 Hudson Street, New York, New York 10014, U.S.A.
Penguin Group (Canada), 90 Eglinton Avenue East, Suite 700, Toronto,
Ontario, Canada M4P 2Y3 (a division of Pearson Penguin Canada Inc.)
Penguin Books Ltd, 80 Strand, London WC2R 0RL, England
Penguin Ireland, 25 St Stephen's Green, Dublin 2, Ireland (a division of Penguin Books Ltd)
Penguin Group (Australia), 250 Camberwell Road,
Camberwell, Victoria 3124, Australia (a division of Pearson Australia Group Pty Ltd)
Penguin Books India Pvt Ltd, 11 Community Centre,
Panchsheel Park, New Delhi—110 017, India
Penguin Group (NZ), Cnr Airborne and Rosedale Roads, Albany, Auckland 1310,
New Zealand (a division of Pearson New Zealand Ltd)
Penguin Books (South Africa) (Pty) Ltd, 24 Sturdee Avenue,
Rosebank, Johannesburg 2196, South Africa

Penguin Books Ltd, Registered Offices: 80 Strand, London WC2R 0RL, England

Text copyright © 2006 by Celeste Davidson Mannis.
Illustrations copyright © 2006 by John O'Brien.
Cover illustration copyright © 2006 by Nancy Harrison.
All rights reserved. Published by Grosset & Dunlap,
a division of Penguin Young Readers Group,
345 Hudson Street, New York, New York 10014.
GROSSET & DUNLAP is a trademark of Penguin Group (USA) Inc.
Printed in the U.S.A.

Library of Congress Control Number: 2006011385

ISBN 0-448-43904-2   10 9 8 7

Contents

Who Was
William Shakespeare?

William Shakespeare—you probably know his name even if you haven't read anything by him yet. He lived four hundred and fifty years ago, wrote at least thirty-five plays, and more than one hundred and fifty poems. Many people think Shakespeare is the greatest playwright who ever lived.

Everything Shakespeare wrote has been translated into dozens of languages, from Spanish to Japanese to Swahili. People all over the world still watch performances of his plays. Movies and Broadway musicals have been based on many of them, such as *Romeo and Juliet, Macbeth,* and *Hamlet.* Hundreds of words and phrases we use every day were invented by him—words like cold-blooded, quarrelsome, and love letter. His language, ideas, and stories are all around us.

Although William Shakespeare is very famous, we don't know a lot about him. Much of his personal life remains a mystery. Back in the 1500s, not many records were kept for the average person. We know Shakespeare began his life as the son of a glove-maker in the small town of Stratford-upon-Avon. He ended it as a rich and famous London playwright. But what happened in between? We know when he married and when he had children. We know he didn't live with his family for many years. Instead, he went to London, where he became an actor, playwright, and a director of plays. He built and bought theaters. He wrote and acted in plays for the Queen of England. He made friends with powerful noble-men.

But what about Shakespeare's day-to-day life? What kind of man and father was he? What made him write plays?

WORDS AND...

HUNDREDS OF WORDS AND PHRASES "COINED"
BY WILLIAM SHAKESPEARE ARE STILL USED TODAY.
HERE ARE JUST A FEW.

AMAZEMENT	OUTGROW
BIRTHPLACE	PUPPY DOG
COLD-BLOODED	QUARRELSOME
DAWN	RASCALLY
EYEBALL	SCHOOLBOY
FASHIONABLE	TRANQUIL
GENEROUS	USEFUL
ILL-TEMPERED	VULNERABLE
JADED	WELL-BEHAVED
LOVE LETTER	YELPING
MAJESTIC	ZANY

PHRASES

"ALL THE WORLD'S A STAGE, AND ALL THE MEN
AND WOMEN MERELY PLAYERS . . ."
—AS YOU LIKE IT

"KNOCK, KNOCK, KNOCK! WHO'S THERE?"
—MACBETH

"NEITHER A BORROWER, NOR A LENDER BE . . ."
—HAMLET

". . . PARTING IS SUCH SWEET SORROW . . ."
—ROMEO AND JULIET

"NEITHER RIME NOR REASON . . ."
— THE COMEDY OF ERRORS

"TO THINE OWN SELF BE TRUE . . ."
—HAMLET

"TOO MUCH OF A GOOD THING . . ."
—AS YOU LIKE IT

"WILD-GOOSE CHASE"
—ROMEO AND JULIET

Chapter 1
Little Will

Baby Will was baptized in Stratford's Holy Trinity Church, in 1564. The exact date of his birth is unknown, but it is celebrated on April 23. In England, that day is also a holiday, filled with playacting and parties. It seems a good day to honor England's greatest playwright as well.

The Shakespeare family lived in Stratford-upon Avon, England, about one hundred miles northwest of London. No more than twenty-five hundred people lived there. When Will was just a few months old, a horrible

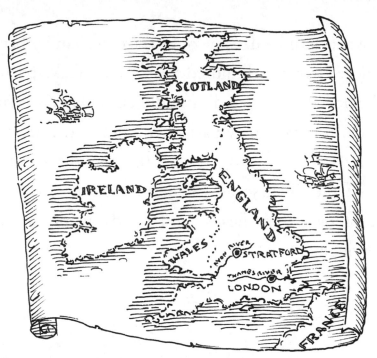

illness swept through the country. It was called the black death, or bubonic plague. Over two hundred people in Stratford died. The very old and very young were hardest hit. Luckily, John and Mary Shakespeare survived. And so did their firstborn son.

Will's father made gloves, belts, purses, and aprons. Will's mother came from a family who owned farmland. She could trace her family back more than five hundred years. The Shakespeares belonged to England's middle class. They weren't rich, nor were they part of the nobility. But they lived well. During the 1560s, English families like the Shakespeares had food on the table, a roof over their heads, and steady work. It was enough.

TYPICAL STRATFORD HOME
OF THE 1500S

By the time Will was born, Elizabeth I had been queen for six years. She was thirty-one years old. She had no interest in war. Under Good Queen Bess, as she was called, England grew more and more prosperous.

It was also a time of discovery and new ideas. In 1519, Ferdinand Magellan, a Portuguese explorer, set out to sail all the way around the world. The trip took three years. It had never been done before.

In 1514, Nicolaus Copernicus, a Polish astronomer, first wrote that the sun was the center of the

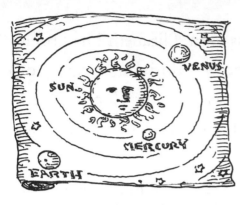

universe. Before that, people believed the earth was the center with the sun and other planets circling around it.

Artists throughout Europe, especially in Italy, were creating some of the most beautiful paintings and sculptures the world has ever known. The printing press, invented in the 1400s, made many more books available. Before that time,

books had to be copied by hand. More and more people learned to read and write.

This was the world that William Shakespeare was born into.

Stratford was a bustling market town on the banks of the Avon River. Crowds came on market day or passed through town on their way to London. What could a person buy? Almost

anything, from pigs and sheep to pretty ribbons, warm woolen clothing, and soft doeskin gloves.

The job of the town council was to keep law and order. John Shakespeare was a member of the town council for many years. When Will was four years old, his father served as high bailiff for a year. It was like being mayor. The position was one of great honor.

As a young boy, Will learned a great deal from plays, poetry, and folktales. They were written and performed by ordinary people on the streets of Stratford—stories about love and great events in history.

Nearby was a town called Coventry. It was famous for mystery plays. These plays were about stories from the Bible. Stages were set up on wagons. A different scene from the mystery play was performed on each wagon as they rolled through town. People came to Coventry from all over to watch. Perhaps little Will traveled there to see them.

Sometimes professional actors came to Stratford.
When Will was four years old, a group called
the Queen's Men visited. The people of Stratford
crowded into the town hall. There they watched
the troupe try out in front of the town council.

Will's father liked the actors. As high bailiff, he
gave them permission to perform in town. He paid
them nine shillings—about fifty dollars—from the

Stratford treasury to put on a show. That was a lot of money then.

After that, groups of actors came more often. Will watched them build stages in the town square and hang thick bolts of fabric for backdrops. They pulled fancy costumes from their trunks. And presto! The play began. Young Will must have been spellbound. Swordfights, battles, love scenes. Tears and laughter. It was pure magic!

Once, Queen Elizabeth visited a nearby castle. Will was eleven. There, actors dressed like knights and princesses. Others dressed like mermaids and imaginary beasts. They roamed the castle gardens or floated in boats on a pond. Still others performed on stages. Music drifted on the warm summer air, and fireworks dazzled the nighttime sky. The festivities went on for weeks.

GOOD QUEEN BESS
1533–1603

QUEEN ELIZABETH I

QUEEN ELIZABETH I WAS GOOD, INDEED! IN FACT, MANY CONSIDER HER ONE OF ENGLAND'S GREATEST RULERS. BORN TO HENRY VIII AND ANNE BOLEYN, ELIZABETH WAS JUST TWO WHEN HER MOTHER WAS BEHEADED FOR TREASON.

ELIZABETH WAS RAISED BY SERVANTS—FAR FROM HER FATHER'S COURT. AN AMAZING STUDENT, SHE STUDIED PHILOSOPHY, RELIGION, AND HISTORY. SHE COULD READ AND WRITE IN SIX DIFFERENT LANGUAGES.

ELIZABETH CAME TO THE THRONE IN 1558, AT THE AGE OF TWENTY-FIVE. SHE NEVER MARRIED, POSSIBLY SO SHE WOULDN'T HAVE TO GIVE UP POWER TO A HUSBAND. SHE HAD LITTLE INTEREST IN MAKING WAR AND HAD A GENUINE LOVE FOR HER PEOPLE. HER PEACEFUL RULE SET THE STAGE FOR AN ERA OF EXPLORATION AND SCIENTIFIC DISCOVERY, AS WELL AS THE BLOSSOMING OF LITERATURE, DRAMA, AND THE FINE ARTS. GOOD QUEEN BESS RULED FOR FORTY-FOUR YEARS.

Some people from Stratford were invited to see the plays at the castle. As a member of the town council, John Shakespeare was probably one of them. Perhaps he took young Will with him. One day, Will would be writing plays for the queen himself. But that day was a long way off.

KING'S NEW SCHOOL

It is likely that Will started school when he was five years old. The King's New School was on the top floor of the Stratford town hall.

School days were long. Will rose before sunrise, ate breakfast, finished his chores, and walked to school. He was at his desk by six o'clock in the morning during the summer, seven o'clock in the winter. School ended at six o'clock in the evening. Classes were held six days a week, all year round. Will's only days off were Sundays, market days, and holidays. In Stratford, as in most of England, school was only for boys.

Will learned to read from a hornbook: a board with the letters of the alphabet and the Lord's Prayer printed on it. He also learned many other prayers.

A year or two later, Will began to read Aesop's *Fables* and Bible stories. He also read comic plays written a thousand years earlier. They were by a playwright named Plautus who lived in ancient Rome.

Learning Latin was very important. Will began studying it when he was seven. Church services were held in Latin. Laws were written in Latin. As Will grew older, he and the other boys were not allowed to speak English at school. Only Latin. They were spanked if they spoke English. Will learned Latin grammar; he knew famous speeches in Latin by heart. He could write in Latin.

Will also performed in plays and had debates with the other boys. He became good at it. He probably liked to be in front of a crowd.

In Shakespeare's plays there are many lines about school. Most of them make school seem like a chore. In one play, *As You Like It*, he describes the "whining school-boy" who is "creeping like snail Unwillingly to school." Does that mean Will didn't like school? Nobody knows. We never can be sure when William Shakespeare's characters are speaking for William Shakespeare, the man.

We do know that Will learned a lot that he used later in his plays. The Bible story of Cain and Abel is mentioned twenty-five times in his work.

CAIN

ABEL

He borrowed funny stories from famous plays he liked, and sad stories, too. In *Romeo and Juliet*, two young people fall in love, but their families are enemies. So Romeo and Juliet get married in secret. But by the end of the play, both are dead. The plot of this play comes from Virgil.

Virgil was a Roman poet who lived sixteen hundred years before William Shakespeare was born. Was it considered cheating to borrow stories? Not at the time. This is what writers often did. What made Shakespeare's plays so great were the characters he created and the beautiful language he used.

Will never went beyond grammar school. That's the reason some people don't believe he wrote the plays. How could he? they ask. A man with so little schooling? Some believe that Christopher Marlowe, a famous playwright of the same time, was really Shakespeare. Still others even suggest that Queen Elizabeth I or a nobleman—the Earl of Oxford—may have written the plays. But grammar school then was very different from elementary school now. By the time Will finished grammar school, he had studied many subjects taught in college today, such as philosophy, history, and great literature.

When Will was thirteen, his family fell on hard times. The wool trade was England's largest industry. In the 1570s it collapsed. When the wool trade suffered, everyone suffered.

Besides being a glover, Will's father was a moneylender. But when times got bad, many people who borrowed money could not pay it back. John was also a brogger. A brogger sold wool

without a proper license. But John no longer made money from his wool business. To make matters worse, Will's father had borrowed money. He stopped going to church because he was afraid to run into people he owed. He stopped going to town council meetings. He sold his wife's land to pay debts. Will's father had risen quickly in the town of Stratford. He fell on hard times just as fast.

There were six children in the Shakespeare family. Will was the oldest and expected to help out at home. We don't know what jobs he took after leaving school. But going on to a university wasn't possible. Money was too tight.

Some historians believe that Will became an assistant teacher. Others think he was a clerk for a lawyer. Will may have been an apprentice in his father's leather business. Apprentices started doing the simplest jobs, like running errands. Training lasted for many years. But is anything known for sure? No! Not until Will turned eighteen.

That's when William Shakespeare married Anne Hathaway.

Chapter 2
Marriage and Children

Anne Hathaway came from the village of Shottery. It was just a short walk across a cornfield from Stratford. Anne was one of seven children. Her family lived in a roomy cottage beside an apple orchard. No one knows how she and Will met. They were married on November 28, 1582. Anne was twenty-six years old. Will

ANNE HATHAWAY'S HOUSE

was only eighteen. He couldn't even apply for a marriage license by himself. His father had to sign the license as well.

What made Will marry a woman so much older? Was he in love? These are more questions with no certain answers. One reason for the wedding may be that Anne was expecting a baby. The newlyweds moved into John and Mary Shakespeare's house on Henley Street. Their daughter Susanna was born six months later. Twins—Hamnet and Judith—came along a few years after that.

HAMNET, JUDITH, AND SUSANNA

The Shakespeare family was still struggling. It was a time of famine. Crops were poor. People went hungry all over England. All told, there were now eleven mouths to feed in the house.

Soon after the twins were born, William Shakespeare left Stratford. His wife and children stayed behind. One story is that Will was kicked out of town for hunting rabbits on a neighbor's land. This story is not hard to believe. There was very little food to go around.

Another story goes that Will may have joined a troupe of actors that had come to Stratford. One of the actors was killed in a fight. So the company was short a man. Maybe Will took his place. This is also not a hard story to believe. We know that Will worked with many of the actors in this troupe later on in

his career. Perhaps this was his best chance to make money for his family.

Still others think Will may have left town for a very different reason. His cousin had been accused of plotting against the queen. He was secretly a Catholic. In England, it was a dangerous time for Catholics. The queen was the head of the Church of England. Catholics were viewed with suspicion. Will's cousin was sent to prison in London and put to death. Will may have also been a secret Catholic. After what happened to his cousin, perhaps he feared for his life. Did he go into hiding? Maybe.

There is no way to know if any of these stories is true. They're just guesses. For the next seven years there is no account of Will. He seems to have disappeared. The years between 1585 and 1592 are called William Shakespeare's lost years.

Chapter 3
Found Again!

Suddenly Will pops up again in 1592. Records tell us that by this time he was settled in London.

Over two hundred thousand people lived in London in 1592. It was one of the greatest cities in Europe. People came to London in droves, mostly from the countryside but also from around the world. London was the center of trade and government in England.

Will was twenty-eight now. After a small town like Stratford, London must have been a shock. Huge brick and marble houses lined the banks of the Thames River. Behind them, many-storied wooden houses jutted out into narrow lanes. They blocked out sunlight and fresh air. Chamber pots, used as toilets, were emptied

from windows into the streets. They formed filthy streams of sewage that stank and made people sick. Rats scurried about, carrying disease wherever they went. London was home to the richest of the rich and the poorest of the poor.

In good weather Queen Elizabeth sailed down the Thames, her beautiful barge aglitter with gold. Commoners like Will gathered on the riverbank to catch a glimpse of the queen. Her hair was as red as flames, her skin as white as chalk. And her

gowns were made of the finest silks and brocades.
Flutes, drums, and trumpets mingled with the
sounds of laughter and the sparkle of sunlit jewels
as she and members of her court sailed by.

Crossing that very same river was London

Bridge—the bridge in the famous nursery rhyme. London Bridge was crowded with shops and narrow houses. The gates on either end were often decorated in a gruesome way. The rotting heads of dead traitors were stuck on poles. "Beware," these hideous heads seemed to say. "Go against the queen and you will pay the price!"

Beyond the bridge, ships rode the river's tide. Traders came to London from all over the world to buy and sell goods—gold from Africa, silks and spices from Venice, tobacco from America, hand-painted wallpaper from China. Everything was for sale in London.

As Will ate supper in crowded inns, he mingled with people from faraway places who had different ideas. Lectures were a popular London

pastime. Will could hear explorers and scientists describe their travels and discoveries. And as he shared glasses of ale with soldiers in noisy taverns, he enjoyed tales of England's recent victory over Spain.

Some people wonder how Will, son of a Stratford glove-maker, could know so much about the world. In William Shakespeare's time, the world came to London.

What Londoners considered entertainment would strike us as very strange. Bearbaiting was quite popular in Shakespeare's London. It was a "blood" sport where bears and dogs fought each other to the death. Public hangings also drew big crowds. People shouted and cheered as the hangman

slipped his noose around the necks of Queen
Elizabeth's enemies.

But nothing was quite as popular as the
theater.

Before Will's day, plays were performed in town
halls, inns, and squares. There were no theaters. But
in 1576, James Burbage did something different.
He was an actor trained as a carpenter. He built the
first theater, called simply the Theatre, just north of
London. The word "theater" comes from *theatron*,
which means "seeing place" in Latin.

Burbage's wooden theater was a circular arena

with an open roof. A giant stage sat in the center of the arena. It was surrounded by galleries on three sides. The galleries had a roof made of thatching—bunches of straw tied together.

The best tickets in the house cost sixpence, or six pennies. That bought a seat with a cushion, but the stage was far away. Will was hardly a rich man. He probably paid about a penny for one of the cheapest tickets. He was allowed to stand with the other *groundlings*, or cheap ticket holders, closest to the stage. There, playgoers enjoyed

snacks such as hazelnuts, oranges, and a drink called mead. They were also quick to toss other foods, like rotten fruit, at bad actors. Will knew it was a play day when a flag was raised outside the theater. Then he, and much of London, came running.

The Lord Mayor of London did not support the theater. Theaters attracted big, noisy crowds that drank too much ale and spread diseases such as the plague. A crowded theater was also a tempting place for pickpockets. The Lord Mayor placed many restrictions on acting troupes. There were rules for when and where they could perform.

Not surprisingly, all the great theaters were built just beyond London's city limits. There, the Lord Mayor's rules didn't matter. He had no power.

Burbage's Theatre was very successful. So another theater sprang up practically next door. It was called the Curtain. Several years later, the Rose was built just south of the Thames. And then a huge theater, called the Swan, was built near the Rose.

The success of the new theaters was largely due to Queen Elizabeth. She loved plays. She often invited acting troupes to perform at court. The queen's love of the theater made it a respectable pastime for all Londoners.

A group of young playwrights, the University Wits, were all the rage in London. They wrote action-packed plays with ancient Greek and Roman settings. There were always lots of complicated plot twists. And the plays were written in a poetic new style. It was called *blank verse*.

Blank verse doesn't rhyme, but it has rhythm. When you clap out a beat or play the drums, you create a rhythm. The rhythm, or pattern, of most blank verse has a fancy name: iambic pentameter. If you were to clap your hands to this rhythm, every other beat would be loud. Like this: da-DUM, da-DUM, da-DUM, da-DUM, da-DUM. This pattern repeats five times in each line of blank verse. Shakespeare used iambic pentameter to make his words flow as gracefully as notes of music.

CHRISTOPHER MARLOWE

Christopher Marlowe was the greatest of the new playwrights at this time. He was born the same year as Will, and he came from the same kind of background. He was the son of a shoemaker. But Marlowe had gone to Cambridge University.

No doubt Will stood in the open courtyard of the Rose theater many times to watch Marlowe's plays. There he had the opportunity to learn much about poetry and playwriting. Later, Will wrote many of his plays in blank verse. He became a master of the style.

Christopher Marlowe and William Shakespeare would have become great rivals in the world of theater. But Marlowe was a short-tempered fellow. He was killed in a tavern brawl in 1593 at the age of twenty-nine.

Of course, Will couldn't just have fun, watching plays in London. He needed to earn a living. His first jobs in the theater probably had very little to do with acting or playwriting.

Theatergoers needed someone to tend their horses. A popular story goes that Will took care of this. In fact, he was so good at the job, he soon

hired boys to help him. Whether this story is true or not, for hundreds of years boys who held this job were known as "Shakespeare's boys." Will may also have sold theater tickets. Or he may have been a prompter's assistant, helping actors with their lines during rehearsals.

At some point, Will did begin to act. He had a lot of talent, but he must have started with small roles.

Life in the theater was hard. It was also not considered a very respectable profession. Troupes were small. There were only eight to twelve players in a troupe. Will would have found himself playing several different roles in each play. All roles, even those of women, were performed by men. Every troupe had a number of different plays they put on. In order to learn his parts, Will studied a scroll with just his lines on it.

It was at this time that Will began to write. At first he probably added lines to other people's plays. He may have reworked old plays to make them seem new. Will also had a very naughty sense of humor. He may have thought up jokes to make the audience laugh.

A different play was performed each afternoon. New plays were rehearsed every morning. Will was hardworking, smart, and versatile.

Soon, he would be famous.

Chapter 4
Upstart Crow

By 1592, Will was the hottest playwright in London. Although Will always kept on acting, his writing made him a star.

That year, Robert Greene, a University Wit, wrote that Will was an "upstart crow." By that, Greene meant that Shakespeare was a common sort of fellow. Somebody who liked making a lot of noise. It was not a very kind or accurate description. But it is the first record we have of Will since 1587.

If anything, William Shakespeare is even more famous now than then. No one can say for sure exactly how many plays he wrote or in what order. Many plays that were once said to be his

THE TWO GENTLEMEN OF VERONA
PROTEUS AND VALENTINE

later turned out to be written by someone else. Most scholars believe he wrote thirty-eight plays.

The Two Gentlemen of Verona is thought to be his first.

Set in Italy, the story is about the adventures of two friends traveling through the country-side. The play is well-written, but very simple, especially compared to his later plays. It was not performed much during his life. That's probably because audiences didn't like it. In the theater, the audience was the ultimate measure of success. Will quickly moved on to plays that people *did* like.

In 1588, the King of Spain had sent a fleet of ships to fight the English. But Spain was defeated.

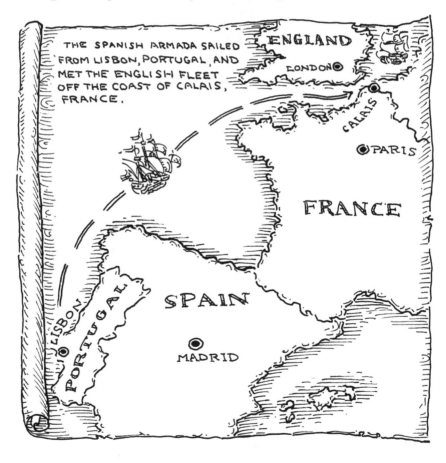

THE SPANISH ARMADA SAILED FROM LISBON, PORTUGAL, AND MET THE ENGLISH FLEET OFF THE COAST OF CALAIS, FRANCE.

ENGLAND

LONDON

CALAIS

PARIS

FRANCE

LISBON

PORTUGAL

SPAIN

MADRID

People in England were proud of their victory. While most other playwrights were busy writing about ancient Greece and Rome, Will wrote a series of plays about English kings and English wars. This was very new, very daring. London went wild.

Written in 1591 and 1592, *Henry VI* (Part I, Part II, and Part III) was set in the 1400s, during the War of the Roses. This war was fought between two powerful and rich English families: the Lancasters and the Yorks. Each family wanted to rule England.

THE SPANISH ARMADA
1588

IN THE SIXTEENTH CENTURY, SPAIN WAS THE
MOST POWERFUL COUNTRY IN THE WORLD. IN 1588
THE SPANISH KING SENT A FLEET, OR ARMADA,
OF HUGE WARSHIPS TO ENGLAND. IT WOULD BE
HIS NEXT CONQUEST! ENGLAND'S SMALL NAVY
MET THE SPANISH IN THE ENGLISH CHANNEL. THE
SPANISH SHIPS WERE BULKY, BUILT TO CARRY
TROOPS AND SUPPLIES TO DISTANT LANDS.
ENGLISH SHIPS WERE SMALLER AND NIMBLE, EASY
TO MANEUVER. CANNON SHOTS BLASTED ACROSS
THE WATER. "FIRE" SHIPS WERE SET ABLAZE AND

AIMED AT THE ENEMY LIKE FLOATING BOMBS. AND
TO TOP IT ALL OFF, A VIOLENT STORM RAGED. THE
SPANISH WERE SURPRISED BY BOTH THE SKILL OF
THE ENGLISH AND THE SUDDEN STORM. MANY OF
THEIR SHIPS WERE SUNK. OTHERS WERE FORCED
AGROUND. STILL OTHERS SCATTERED. ENGLAND
WAS SAVED! IT WAS THE FIRST GREAT NAVAL
BATTLE WON BY THE ENGLISH. AFTER THAT TIME,
THE ENGLISH RULED THE SEAS FOR SEVERAL
HUNDRED YEARS.

Will's plays about English kings were full of battle scenes and action. But he also made audiences think about what power does to people and why wars start. He did so by looking at what had happened in his very own country. The plays did not take place in a distant time or far-off place. Why was this such a bold thing to do? In these plays, kings were treated as people, not godlike, all-powerful rulers. What if Queen Elizabeth took offense? More than a few people who displeased the queen ended up with their heads decorating London Bridge. But the plays were a smashing success.

In *Richard III*, Shakespeare went even further. He wrote about an English ruler who was evil through and through. So evil that he killed his own brother and young nephews in order to become king. Yet the wicked, hunchbacked Richard III was one of Will's first great characters. Why?

Wicked as he is, Richard seems very human.

By the time the play is over, Shakespeare actually makes the audience feel sorry for him. In the last act of the play, Richard has lost everything. He has even lost his mind. He thinks he is in the middle of a terrible battle, with no horse, and no way to escape. He runs around the stage shouting, "A horse! A horse! My kingdom for a horse!"

"A HORSE ! A HORSE !
MY KINGDOM FOR A HORSE !"

King Richard sees how much bloodshed he has caused. And it is too much for him to bear. He wants to escape from the nightmare he has created. Now he is even willing to give up his kingdom to do so.

Shakespeare's characters are what make his plays so interesting. Some are mostly evil, with a kernel of good or regret in them. Others are mostly good, but with a flaw in their personalities that leads them to ruin their own lives and the lives of those they love. He was the first to make characters as complicated as real people. After watching one of his plays, the audience would leave thinking about why people do the things they do.

His plays were popular because he also appealed to popular taste. He understood what entertained people. *Titus Andronicus* is a bloodthirsty story about ancient Rome. The action is a lot like that in modern war movies. One side, the Romans, are "good guys." Their enemies, the Goths, are "bad guys." But as the story moves forward, we see good and bad in both sides. War is not simple. By the end of the play, almost every character is dead. Titus has gone mad. He serves his archenemy a pie made of the blood and bones of her sons. *Titus Andronicus* is not considered one of Shakespeare's great plays. But London audiences ate it up!

Many of Will's plays are funny—and Londoners loved to have a good laugh. In one of his first comedies, *The Taming of the Shrew*, Will explored another kind of war. Petruchio, a fortune hunter, marries a rich woman named Kate. She is a "shrew," sharp-tongued and hot tempered. Kate has a mind of her own, and she speaks it. She is strong, stubborn, and intelligent. She can also be cruel. Petruchio

doesn't care. He is confident he can "tame" her and turn her into a model wife.

Petruchio comes to his wedding in rags. He drags Kate away to his home during the wedding party. He won't let her sleep or eat. He treats her harshly in order to break her spirit.

In Elizabethan England, men were considered better than women. For years, the play was thought to be nothing more than a comedy that mirrored beliefs about how women in the 1500s should behave. But is it?

After *The Taming of the Shrew*, Will wrote several plays with very strong women characters, like Cleopatra, Queen of Egypt. This was unusual. Even the brilliant playwright Christopher Marlowe never wrote good roles for female characters. Yet a woman was the strongest, most powerful person in England. Queen Elizabeth I never chose to get married and certainly was never "tamed" by any man. Is it possible Will was making fun of the way men thought of women in his time? We don't know. But we do know that Will explored many serious issues in this play, even if they are wrapped up in a story full of comic twists and turns.

Tragedy. Comedy. History. William Shakespeare could write anything. Audiences were crazy about the plays. Nothing could stop the newest talent on the London theater scene.

Except the Black Death.

THE BLACK DEATH

IT SOUNDS TERRIBLE, AND IT WAS. HORRIBLE PURPLISH-BLACK BOILS GAVE THE DEADLY BUBONIC PLAGUE ITS NICKNAME. THEY WERE ONE OF THE FIRST SIGNS OF THE DISEASE. IN A FEW DAYS MOST VICTIMS WERE DEAD.

PLAGUE FIRST TRAVELED TO EUROPE FROM ASIA IN 1348. IT WAS CARRIED BY FLEAS THAT LIVED IN THE FUR OF RATS AND OTHER SMALL ANIMALS. WITHIN THREE YEARS, IT KILLED OVER

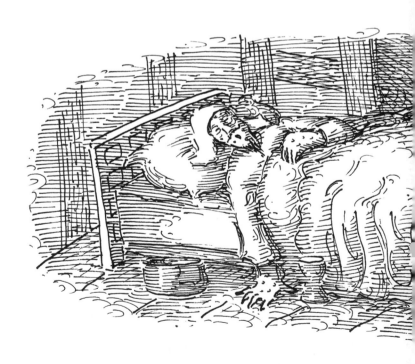

TWENTY MILLION PEOPLE—ALMOST A THIRD OF THE ENTIRE POPULATION OF EUROPE. PLAGUE SWEPT SHAKESPEARE'S ENGLAND SEVERAL TIMES. VICTIMS' HOMES WERE LOCKED, BOLTED, AND NAILED SHUT. NO ONE COULD COME IN OR GO OUT. WHOLE FAMILIES AND TOWNS WERE WIPED OUT IN THIS WAY.

Chapter 5
The Plague and a Patron

Between June of 1592 and April of 1594, bubonic plague swept through London. It claimed over two hundred thousand lives. Theaters were shut down as the deadly disease spread like wildfire.

The filthy, crowded city was a breeding ground
for disease. Many people fled to the countryside.

Many acting troupes split up or went to other towns. There was no need for new plays.

Will probably left London, too. He didn't return to Stratford; nobody knows where he went. However, we do know what he did during this time of plague. William Shakespeare took quill in hand and wrote poetry.

Venus and Adonis was Will's first published poem. It was about the romance between the goddess of love and a shy young mortal. The

story came from the Roman poet Ovid. Will's next poem was about the Trojan War. Both were published by Richard Field, a printer originally from Stratford.

The poems were dedicated to an important nobleman, the Earl of Southampton. He liked the poems and became Will's patron. He gave Will money so he could spend all his time writing.

EARL OF SOUTHAMPTON

To add to Will's good fortune, a famous London publisher, John Harrison, bought both poems from the first publisher. Will's reputation grew. He had started as a mere playwright. Now he was taken seriously as a poet.

Will also began to write sonnets at this time. Sonnets are fourteen-line poems with complicated rhyme patterns. Many of Will's sonnets were about a mysterious dark lady. But to this day no one knows who the dark lady was. Was she a real woman? Or did she exist only in Will's imagination? Over the years, many scholars have wondered how closely the sonnets reflect Shakespeare's own experiences. The tone of many of them is very personal. How exciting it would be to find clues about the man in his lines of poetry.

Will wrote 154 sonnets over the years. When he was forty-five years old, they were published as a collection. Books of his sonnets are still in print.

Then, in the spring of 1594, London theaters

reopened. Actors returned to the city. Old acting troupes reunited. New ones formed. After two years of sickness and empty theaters, excitement crackled in the air.

Will couldn't stay away.

Chapter 6
The Chamberlain's Men

In London, Will joined an acting group: the Lord Chamberlain's Men. With the money from his poetry, he became a part owner of the company. He helped pay for scripts, costumes, and sets. In return, he kept some of the profits from ticket sales. Plays were put on at the Theatre and sometimes at court for the queen.

Will threw himself into the art, craft, and business of theater. He would remain with this

troupe of actors for the rest of his career. That would be close to twenty years.

During this time, Shakespeare wrote some of his best early plays. The tragedy *Romeo and Juliet* and the comedy *A Midsummer Night's Dream* are the two most famous. Both are romantic stories with poetic language.

In *Romeo and Juliet,* the story of the unlucky lovers ends in tragedy. In *A Midsummer Night's Dream* romance takes a fanciful turn. One summer's night, two sets of lovers fall under the spell of forest fairies. The complicated plot includes a bickering fairy king and queen, a mischievous pixie called Puck, love potions, and a man who magically turns into a donkey!

A string of successes marked the years from 1594 to 1596. In the summer of 1596, Will and the Lord Chamberlain's Men went on tour in the countryside south of London.

In the midst of this busy, happy time, tragedy struck. Hamnet, Will's eleven-year-old son, died.

Will had been living apart from his wife and children for a long time. He may have visited them once or twice a year. But he never stopped taking care of his family. Hamnet's death must have been a terrible blow.

Much of Will's work after Hamnet's death is filled with heartache and longing. Did Will regret leaving his family behind?

Hamnet's death came at a time when money was no longer a problem for Will. The following year, in the spring, Will bought a pretty house for his family. It was called New Place, on Chapel Street in Stratford. Made of brick and timber, it was the second largest in town. Will paid a great deal of money for it. How sad that Hamnet was not there to enjoy the Shakespeares' beautiful new home.

NEW PLACE

Will also helped out his father. John Shakespeare wanted a coat of arms. A coat of arms was a status symbol. It meant a person was a "gentleman." Will helped his father apply for one. And John Shakespeare was granted a coat of arms.

COAT OF ARMS

IT WASN'T ENOUGH TO BE WELL OFF IN SHAKESPEARE'S ENGLAND. MEN WANTED TO "MOVE UP" IN SOCIAL CLASS. THEY WANTED TO BE THOUGHT OF AS GENTLEMEN. ONE WAY TO DO THIS WAS TO ACQUIRE A COAT OF ARMS. IT WAS A SHIELD-SHAPED DESIGN THAT BORE A FAMILY MOTTO. THE MOTTO ON THE SHAKESPEARE FAMILY CREST READS: *NON SANZ DROICT*, LATIN FOR "NOT WITHOUT RIGHT." A COAT OF ARMS WAS USUALLY GRANTED BASED ON FAMILY BACKGROUND AND NOBLE DEEDS. BUT SOMETIMES THEY WERE BOUGHT AT A HIGH PRICE.

ONCE JOHN SHAKESPEARE WAS GRANTED A COAT OF ARMS, HE COULD PASS IT DOWN TO WILL AND FUTURE GENERATIONS OF SHAKESPEARES.

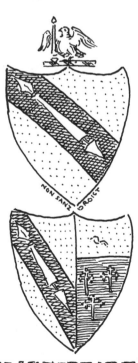

SHAKESPEARE'S COAT OF ARMS

At the same time that Anne and the children settled into their new house, Will's theater troupe was kicked out of theirs. The landlord was demanding a huge increase to rent the land on which the Theatre stood.

It didn't seem fair. The troupe had always paid their rent. They owned the Theatre. But they just did not own the land it sat on. The troupe tried to strike a deal with the landlord. They held out for as long as they could. But the landlord wouldn't budge. So the actors packed up their costumes and scenery and moved to the nearby Curtain. They weren't very happy about it. But for now, it would have to do.

The playhouse wasn't all they lost. James Burbage, who had built and run the Theatre, died in 1597. But James's sons filled their father's shoes and kept the company running. And William Shakespeare wrote one hit play after another. Again, some were about very hot topics.

In 1594, the queen's doctor was accused of trying to poison her. He was dragged through the streets and killed in front of a laughing crowd.

The doctor was Jewish. His brutal death may have inspired Will to write *The Merchant of Venice*.

In the play, a young man borrows money from a Jewish moneylender named Shylock. Shylock demands a pound of a man's flesh if he is not repaid. Shylock is portrayed as being greedy, cruel, and unfeeling. At the time, this was what many people believed about Jews. Shakespeare, however, shows the audience that Shylock, despite his flaws, is a human being like any other. This was something new for the times. In a famous speech, Shylock says, "I am a Jew. Hath not a Jew eyes? . . . If you prick us, do we not bleed? If you tickle us, do we not laugh? If you poison us, do we not die? And if you wrong us, shall we not seek revenge?"

SHYLOCK

Other characters who first appear to be fine, upstanding citizens prove to be cruel and unjust. Once again Shakespeare reveals to the audience that nothing in life is clear and simple.

At around the same time, Will turned to English

history again, with a series of plays about Henry IV, a weak ruler, and his wild son Prince Harry.

The most interesting character in these plays, however, is neither the king nor the prince. It is a lying, cheating, drunken old knight by the name of John Falstaff. Falstaff is considered the greatest comic role ever created by William Shakespeare, possibly the greatest comic role ever. Through Falstaff, William Shakespeare once again wraps very serious ideas in laughter.

Legend has it that Queen Elizabeth enjoyed the character of Falstaff so much that she asked Will to write a play all about him.

He did.

In *The Merry Wives of Windsor*, Falstaff romances two married ladies at the same time. There are plenty of naughty jokes in this play, the kind Shakespeare was famous for. The ladies find out what Falstaff is up to and punish him. He is thrown into a river with the laundry. He is made to dress up like an old woman. He gets chased through a forest by children dressed as ghosts and goblins. Finally he mends his ways.

Will was a master at writing exciting plots. Then, in the winter of 1598, the Chamberlain's Men carried out a daring act themselves, one that caught London by surprise.

Chapter 7
The Globe

Just before Christmas in 1598, Will and the troupe gathered at the empty Theatre. The land wasn't theirs, but the building was—every last board and nail of it! By moonlight, workmen began to take apart the Theatre. Over the next few weeks it was brought across the river, piece by piece. The wood was used to build a new theater in Southwark, near the Rose. Just three months later, the work was done. A new theater arose from the old one.

The stage was framed with rich hangings and held up by giant wooden pillars painted to look like marble. The *heaven*, or top level of the stage, was decorated with angels and clouds. A trapdoor

REBUILDING THE GLOBE

on the main level of the stage allowed actors to appear and disappear, as if by magic. For the grand opening of the new theater, a flag with the Greek hero Hercules on it was flown. On play days, different colored flags flapped merrily in the breeze. A black flag announced a tragedy, white a comedy, and red a history play.

The new theater was named the Globe.

THE GLOBE

THE GLOBE THEATER

IN 1613, A CANNONBALL WAS FIRED ON THE
STAGE OF THE GLOBE DURING A PERFORMANCE
OF HENRY VIII. SPARKS LIT THE THATCHED ROOF
OF THE THEATER. PLAYGOERS AND ACTORS FLED.
THE STRUCTURE WAS ENGULFED IN FLAMES. NO
ONE WAS HURT, BUT THE THEATER BURNED TO THE
GROUND. WITHIN A YEAR, THE GLOBE WAS REBUILT.

One of the first plays performed at the Globe was *Julius Caesar*. It is about the most powerful emperor of ancient Rome. In the play, men close to Caesar plot to kill him and take power. As in many of William Shakespeare's plays, *Julius Caesar* shows just how attractive and dangerous power can be. We see how far some people will go to gain it.

In Shakespeare's time, there was a similar plot to strip power from Queen Elizabeth. Queen Elizabeth never married. But there were rumors that the aging queen and the handsome young Earl of Essex were in love.

Then in 1601, Essex planned a coup, or rebellion. Essex wanted to be king himself.

Right before the coup, a group of Essex's friends visited the Globe. They asked the Chamberlain's Men to perform *Richard II*. It was one of Will's earlier plays, not one of his most popular. But they offered Will and the troupe a lot of money. Why did Essex want people to see this play?

EARL OF ESSEX

Richard II was the story of a weak English king who is forced to give up his throne. Essex wanted the crowd of almost three thousand people to think about rebellion. He even planted people to shout and clap during certain scenes. They were the scenes making fun of the king. The idea was to stir up the audience against Queen Elizabeth. But Elizabeth uncovered the plot. Essex was thrown into prison. He and most of his men were executed.

Will and the Chamberlain's Men were questioned. Did they know about the plot? Were they in on it? Why did they agree to put on *Richard II*? Their answers must have sounded like the truth. In the end, the troupe was sent home. No one was punished. But the event showed how dangerous putting on a play could be.

Queen Elizabeth was an old woman by this time. At sixty-nine years old, she had been queen for forty-three years. As she grew older, the way she looked and dressed became more and more outrageous. Her face was thickly painted with white makeup. A bright red wig covered her thin gray hair. Her gowns were made of gold and silver cloth. Diamonds, rubies, sapphires, and pearls were sewn onto them. Jewels often fell off her

gowns and littered the floors of her chambers.

And Queen Elizabeth was still unmarried. Why was this such an important issue? It wasn't simply because people were interested in her love life. Once a king or queen died, usually the eldest son became the next ruler. But Elizabeth had no sons. She had no children. And she refused to pick an heir. Someone to rule after her. The queen wasn't going to live forever. What would happen after she died? These years were filled with uncertainty and trouble for most people.

Then in 1601, England was gripped by famine and plague again. William Shakespeare, however, was growing richer and more famous. He'd been writing hit plays for ten years. He was making a small fortune as a part owner of the Globe. He was also buying farmland in the countryside around Stratford.

At this time Will wrote *Hamlet*, the first of four great tragedies. (He wrote it around the same time that his father died.)

Hamlet is considered one of William Shakespeare's masterpieces. The story is about a young prince whose father, the king of Denmark, has been murdered. Who is the killer? The king's own brother—Hamlet's uncle! The uncle then marries Hamlet's mother and becomes the new king.

At the beginning of the play, the ghost of Hamlet's father appears and demands that his son avenge the murder. (Shakespeare himself may have played the ghost.) But Hamlet can't bring himself

to do it. Instead, Hamlet spends the greater part of the play pretending to be crazy. It's his way of avoiding taking action. He roams about the castle talking to himself.

In a play, solo speeches are called soliloquies. Only the audience hears the speech—no other characters. In his soliloquies, Hamlet reveals his inner feelings. As he talks to himself, he asks the great questions of the play. What does it mean to be a human being? What responsibilities do we have? To ourselves? To our country?

At one point Hamlet feels so hopeless, he considers killing himself. In a famous soliloquy, Hamlet says, "To be, or not to be: that is the question . . ." In other words, he is wondering whether "to live or to die." He cannot even make up his mind about that!

William Shakespeare's Hamlet is a tragic hero. It is also interesting how close his name is to Hamnet, Shakespeare's son. Hamlet is a noble man. He cares deeply about what is right and what is wrong. But in Shakespeare's greatest plays, every tragic hero has a flaw. For Hamlet it is indecision. And this flaw leads to tragedy.

With its dark themes, *Hamlet* is a hard play to watch. But it was a big hit right away. And for the past four hundred years, every great actor has longed to play the part.

In the next five years, Will wrote three more great tragedies: *Othello*, *King Lear*, and *Macbeth*.

Othello is the story of a general who marries a highborn young woman. Her name is Desdemona. Her father is furious because the marriage was performed in secret and the groom is a black man. So once again, Shakespeare stirred up controversy.

Unlike Hamlet, Othello is a man of action. He has great charm, power, and integrity. He loves his new wife. But he is jealous. That is his flaw. One of Othello's soldiers wants to destroy Othello. He convinces Othello that Desdemona is in love with another man. Blinded by jealousy, Othello strikes out, and his actions lead to tragedy.

Othello was a huge hit, too. Will's characters and exciting story thrilled the audience. They also made people think about the terrible nature of prejudice and jealousy.

In February of 1603, Queen Elizabeth died.

She had ruled England for almost half a century.

In dramatic fashion, Elizabeth was on her deathbed before she named the next ruler. It was her cousin James, King of Scotland. Now he became James I of England.

James was a theater lover, too. As king, one of his first acts was to change the name of the Chamberlain's Men. Will's troupe now became known as the King's Men. It was a great honor. The King's Men was the most famous group of actors in all of England.

Shakespeare's next play was set in Scotland, which is north of England. The play was called *Macbeth*. It is full of magic and murder. Returning home from battle, the noble soldier Macbeth meets three witches. They make predictions about his future. One is that Macbeth will become the king of Scotland. Macbeth doesn't believe the witches. But then their predictions start to come true.

Macbeth tells his wife about the witches. Lady Macbeth is very hungry for power. She wants her husband to kill the king. Then he can take over the throne. He does. But once in power, Macbeth and his wife are tortured by guilt.

Lady Macbeth slowly loses her mind. At night she sleepwalks through the castle.

She tries to rub an imaginary spot of blood from her hands. But she cannot wipe away her crimes. Neither can her husband. They are both destroyed by greed and ambition.

How daring of Shakespeare to write a play about a Scottish king who is a murderer. Remember, King James was also the ruler of Scotland. When he came to the throne, the people of England were hopeful. Perhaps there would be more religious freedom. After all, James had a Catholic wife. But just the opposite happened. There were even harsher punishments for anyone defying the Church of England. Many Catholics were shocked and angry.

The Gunpowder Plot caused a big bang the very next year. In 1605, a group of Catholic noblemen planned to kill the king. They were going to blow up a building when the king was inside giving a speech. The plot was foiled, but King James was shaken. Clearly, he was not as popular as he thought. Ripples of discontent spread throughout the country.

That year, William Shakespeare wrote *King Lear*. What is the connection? Once again, he created a play about a king and his misuse of power.

King Lear is very old when the play opens. He decides to leave his kingdom to his three daughters. But first, each daughter must tell him just how much she loves him. He wants to hear that his children love him more than anybody else in the world.

Lear's two older daughters fill his ears with flattery. They do this because they want Lear's land. Not because they love him. His youngest daughter, Cordelia, loves her father very much. But she refuses to play this game of flattery. Lear is furious. Cordelia will get nothing and is banished from the land.

By the time Lear realizes which daughter truly loves him, it is too late. Cordelia is dead. His other daughters turn on him. Lear, now out of his mind, dies of a broken heart. By hearing and seeing only what he wants to, Lear has brought his kingdom to the edge of chaos.

King Lear was written at the peak of Will's career. Soon after Will finished it, there was more happiness and success. His favorite daughter, Susanna, was married. A year after that, in 1608, Will and six other men bought another theater in London. This theater was smaller than the Globe, but it was an indoor theater. The Globe had to close during the winter. Now, William Shakespeare's plays were performed to packed houses all year long.

Chapter 8
Home Again

William Shakespeare continued to write plays for another five years. But in 1610, after more than twenty years in London, Will returned home to his family in Stratford. The plays he created at

this time often deal with families torn apart and then reunited.

At New Place, Will wrote *The Tempest*. It is the last play he wrote alone. And it is the only one where he didn't borrow the plot. He came up with the story all by himself.

A duke named Prospero has been tricked by his brother and cast out to sea. After a terrible storm, Prospero's boat is shipwrecked. He and his daughter, Miranda, find themselves on the shores of a strange, enchanted island.

Through magic, Prospero takes control of the island from a wicked witch. And there he and his child live, befriended by magic spirits and creatures. Prospero's brother comes to the island after many years, and in the last act all is forgiven.

At the very end of *The Tempest*, Prospero comes on stage and begs to be set free from the enchanted island. It is as if William Shakespeare, too, is saying that he has lived a lifetime in a magical place—the make-believe world of theater. But now it is time for him to go. Surrounded by family, William Shakespeare died in 1616, in Stratford, at the age of fifty-two.

Today, almost four hundred years after his death, Shakespeare's work lives on. Although we do not know many details about his personal life, his plays and poetry tell us so much about the mind

DELACORTE THEATER, CENTRAL PARK

and heart of this genius. William Shakespeare's words make us laugh and cry. And perhaps most importantly, they make us dream.

TIMELINE OF SHAKESPEARE'S LIFE

1564	William Shakespeare born
1582	Shakespeare marries Anne Hathaway
1583	Susanna Shakespeare born
1585	Twins Judith and Hamnet Shakespeare born
1587	Beginning of Shakespeare's lost years
1590	*The Two Gentlemen of Verona*
1591	*The Taming of the Shrew*
1595	*Romeo and Juliet; A Midsummer Night's Dream*
1596	Hamnet Shakespeare dies
1596–97	*The Merchant of Venice*
1597–98	*The Merry Wives of Windsor*
1599	Globe Theater built; *Julius Caesar*
1600–01	*Hamlet*
1601	John Shakespeare dies
1603	Chamberlain's Men become King's Men
1605–06	*King Lear*
1606	*Macbeth*
1607	Susanna Shakespeare marries
1609	Shakespeare's *Sonnets* published
1611	*The Tempest*
1613	Old Globe Theater burns down
1616	Judith Shakespeare marries; William Shakespeare dies

TIMELINE OF THE WORLD

Elizabeth I takes the throne	1559
Church of England established	1563
Chinese population reaches sixty million	1578
Francis Drake circles the globe	1580
American colony of Virginia named after Elizabeth I	1587
England defeats the Spanish Armada	1588
Plague in England	1593
Essex rebellion	1601
Queen Elizabeth dies	1603
James VI of Scotland becomes James I of England	1603
Plague in England	1603
First Kabuki theater in Japan	1603
Gunpowder Plot in England	1605
Plague in England	1608
Nursery rhyme "Three Blind Mice" published	1609
Virginia colonists export tobacco	1612
Hot chocolate introduced to Europe	1615
First black slaves arrive in Virginia colony	1619

BIBLIOGRAPHY

The books with a star are for young readers.

*Aagesen, Colleen and Margie Blumberg. **Shakespeare for Kids, His Life and Times.** Chicago, Chicago Review Press, 1999.

*Aliki. **William Shakespeare & the Globe.** New York, HarperCollins, 1999.

*Chrisp, Peter. **Eyewitness Books: Shakespeare.** New York, DK Publishing, 2002.

Dobson, Michael, and Stanley Wells. **The Oxford Companion to Shakespeare.** Oxford, Oxford University Press, 2001.

Greenblatt, Stephen. **Will in the World.** New York, W. W. Norton & Company, 2004.

Macrone, Michael. **Brush Up on Your Shakespeare.** New York, Harper and Row, 1990.

Rowse, A. L. **Shakespeare the Man.**
New York, St. Martin's Press, 1989.

Schoenbaum, S. **William Shakespeare: A Compact Documentary Life.** New York, Oxford University Press, 1987.

*Stanley, Diane. **Bard of Avon.** New York, Morrow Junior Books, 1992.

Wells, Stanley and Gary Taylor, eds. **The Oxford Shakespeare: The Complete Works.** New York, Oxford University Press, 2005.

Websites:

Folger Library:
www.folger.edu

Shakespeare Birthplace Trust:
www.shakespeare.org.uk